Time to Soar

To Sarah ~
may AbunDance
be yours!
♥Katie

Time to Soar: Word Dances and Bird Songs for Every Season

Website: worddances.com

"Embrace" and "Birds of a Feather" first published in *Northern Narratives* — Fargo Public Library

First Edition 2024
Printed in the United States of America

Library of Congress Control Number: 2024901075

ISBN 979-8218301811

Time to Soar

Word Dances and Bird Songs for Every Season

Katie Bruckbauer

Illustrated by Mary Jo Savageau

For Kellie, Philip, and Danny.

May you never forget your roots.
May you always trust your wings.

Contents

I once asked a bird,
"How is it that you fly in this gravity of darkness?"
She responded, "Love lifts me."

~ Hafez

Prologue

The Year of the Bird

A time of upheaval, to put into words,
"This year was strictly for the birds!"

The reason, the albatross Covid-19,
unleashing problems before unseen.

Closures, quarantines, strict isolation,
zoom meetings, zoom parties, zoom education;

medical mysteries, economic devastation,
family feuds and fragmentation.

So much illness, loved ones lost,
the world in turmoil, bearing the cost,

anger, frustration, anxieties stirred.
Did you want to flip this debacle the bird?

Or did you too hear a longing call
to somehow rise above it all,

to leave your nest, to fly away
to somewhere far beyond the fray,

to soar up high for a bird's eye view?
Where's all this going? Sure wish I knew!

But fight or flight is no long-term solution.
It just fills the world with more pollution.

And so I embarked on another path
to bring me through the fear and wrath.

I used this time for pause, reflection.
Our fine-feathered friends my source of connection.

They brought entertainment, exhilaration,
adoration, and inspiration.

The nest of twigs, with eggs safely holding,
awaiting new hatchlings with wings for unfolding;

the owl in his wisdom, the swan with her beauty,
the sparrow so humble, the chickadee cutie;

the dark-eyed junco so full of spunk,
lifting me out of my winter funk;

the cardinals reminding of parents who've passed,
whose love is still with me, a love that will last;

the hawk and the dove, both alive within,
the one that I nurture, the one that will win.

All of them spoke to me, helped me to cope
when I was despairing and searching for hope.

I listened and learned and put into words
the messages given by all of these birds:

Whether it's joys or trials you face,
the season you're in is the one to embrace.

Keep alert. Keep watching and waking.
The lessons are here—here for the taking.

Keep singing your songs and trusting your wings.
Yes, love will lift you whatever life brings.

Spring

Holy Shit

Holy Shit!
An oxymoron.

Or is it?

Clouds

Flying through clouds
of endless gray,
turbulence seems
determined to stay.

Remember the recent
flight, my love,
as you entered a cloud
and looked above?

The sun was shining.
The sky was blue.
Mostly unseen, but
you saw it. You knew.

Then through the mist,
when your eyes gazed down,
you saw the earth,
the solid ground.

You were at peace
in the midst of that storm;
tossed in the turmoil,
but safe and warm.

Hold onto that thought
when you can't find your way
through the sadness and fear
you can't seem to allay.

Remember the blue,
the solid earth,
the love that sustained you
from your birth.

Remember, my child,
life's not all that it seems;
so hold onto the hope,
and hold onto your dreams.

Hope

Once you came to me
as an eagle,
soaring above
my heavenward gaze.
My heart leapt,
and I wept
tears of joy,
amazed that my despair
was not the final word.
That day I made a vow
to find you
somewhere,
somehow;
and you found me.
If it could happen then,
it could happen again.
Hope,
I'm searching now.
Find me
somehow.

Robin

Up here in the north—
where the cold winds blow,
and all the long winter
ice and snow
cover the earth,
keeping us captive
inside our homes,
cooped up and inactive—
signs of spring
are long awaited,
especially in years
when the thaw is belated.
And so when the robins
appear on the scene,
hopping on lawns
that have yet to turn green,
we join their sweet song
and run to remind
our loved ones that spring
won't be too far behind!

Bird Feeder

What could be sweeter than birds at my feeder?
Cardinal, grosbeak, sparrow, and then,
chickadee, nuthatch, finch, and a wren,
swooping in from oak tree or cedar,
me at my window, pausing to greet her (or him),
"Hello pretty tweeter! How have you been?
You bring such joy! Come back again!"

Rose-Breasted Grosbeak

A grosbeak's beak is broad and tri-
angular. I'll tell you why.
It comes in handy when he feeds
on insects, fruits, and hard-shelled seeds.

A grosbeak's streak is rosy-red
upon white breast, but not his head,
so black as black as black can be,
with wings of black-white feathery.

A female grosbeak's meek and pale
with brownish feathers, head, and tail.
A golden tone colors her breast.
She's safe, unseen, upon her nest.

A grosbeak's speak is sweet and clear,
a rambling song that brings good cheer.
With voice and plumage so exquisite,
what a treat when grosbeaks visit!

American Goldfinch

Ah! Goldfinch! Sunny fellow!
Tiny gift of joy
wrapped up in brilliant yellow!

Woodpecker

Hey Mr. Woodpecker!
  Peck peck peck!
I just need to
  check check check.
How's the state of your
  neck neck neck?
And one more thing. What the
  heck heck heck
have you done to my brand new
  deck deck deck?!

Nest

I am safe here
encircled, enclosed
in this abode
of twig, mud, leaf.
It's my belief
there's something more...

But I'm safe here
ringed in love.
Do I dare
step over the rim,
go out on a limb,
explore?

I am safe here.
The world is big.
I am small.
But I have wings
and songs to sing...

Time to soar!

Uplift

I
Call
Upon
You

Lift
Me
Up

Up
Lift
Me

Up
Upon
The
Heights

Summer

Abun*dance*

With more than a glance,
I contemplate life's bounty
and vast variety!

Could it be, perchance,
I have all I need as well,
right here, inside of me?

In every circumstance
I'm given the grace I need, if
I've only eyes to see.

And so I change my stance.
I've had enough of not enough
and high anxiety.

I bravely join the dance.
Moving to the drum within—
trustful, grateful, free.

Hummingbird

Hum-diddy-dum
Hummingbird come
Bring your friends
Bring your daughter
Come and drink our
Sugar water
Hum-diddy-dum
Hummingbird come

Orioles

Do orioles eat Oreos
single-stuffed or double?
Do orioles chew Orbit gum
or opt for ones that bubble?

Do orioles order out
for Prego or Ragu
over orecchiette pasta
or organic orzo stew?

Or what about Ore-Ida Taters,
hash browned or french fried?
An omelet with oregano?
Or eggs cooked sunny side?

Oh my goodness! No no no!
An oriole would never
overdose on Orville
Redenbacher's Popcorn ever!

But an oriole will orient
'round oranges or grape jelly.
Ordinarily, that's what he'd
choose to fill his belly!

Buddy

(for Natalie, Charlotte, and Alaina)

She found him on the ground
alone,
still too young
to live on his own.

She scooped him up,
held him close to her chest,
her small hands forming a
human nest.

"Where are your parents?
Are you hurt? Poor thing!
Have you been abandoned?
Have you broken your wing?

Or have you not yet
learned how to fly?
Don't be frightened.
Don't be shy.

I'll be gentle.
You're safe here with me.
I'll feed and protect you,
I'll name you Buddy."

So feed him she did,
digging worms from the ground,
hour upon hour,
sunup to sundown.

In her care, Buddy grew.
In her care, Buddy thrived!
First one week, then two...
that bird, still alive!

The fledgling she'd rescued
and loved as her own
was learning new skills,
was almost full grown!

He could find his own food.
He had wings for a reason.
The ending was near
for this nurturing season.

Buddy was ready
to take to the air,
but would he be safe
when she wasn't there?

Could she open her hands?
Could she loosen her hold?
Could she let him go free?
Let his own life unfold?

He was not hers to keep.
He was not hers to own.
She would trust and not fear
his future unknown.

With an ache in her chest
and a tear in her eye,
she opened her heart
and let her love fly.

Blue Jay

Hey! Blue Jay, Hey!
So stunning in blue and gray.
In your treetop dwelling,
you're smart and compelling.
I love to watch you play!

Hey! Blue Jay, Hey!
You've sure got a lot to say!
I don't mind you telling,
but please, stop the yelling!
You're spoiling the beautiful day!

Swans

A single swan,
such beauty, grace.
Her silhouette an S.
Is anything more lovely?
Most definitely, yes!

A pair of swans
in love, embrace.
Their silhouette a heart.
Is anything more lovely?
In awe, behold God's art!

Uncommon Common Loon

What an uncommon bird,
the common loon,
with sleek, black head
and eyes maroon,
pinstriped collar,
white and black,
polka-dot sides,
checkerboard back.

What an uncommon bird,
the common loon,
an excellent swimmer,
on land a buffoon.
With legs so close
to his derrière,
walking is awkward.
It's water or air.

What an uncommon bird,
the common loon,
calling to friends
by the light of the moon,
with a wavering wail,
a tense tremolo,
an eerie yodel,
a haunting hello.

What an uncommon bird,
the common loon,
so cautious 'round humans
on boat or pontoon.
So gaze from afar,
respect the space
of the common loon
with the uncommon grace.

Two Birds

Two birds dwelling deep within;
one coos, one squawks.
Who will have dominion—
the white dove, or the hawk?

They're settled and established.
Their nests are built to stay.
The one I feed and nourish
will have the final say.

Hawk is hate personified.
She's always seeking prey.
To keep herself protected,
violence wins the day.

Feed her with a feast of fear,
a plate of puffed-up pride,
self-righteous indignation,
she'll feel justified.

Entrées of green envy,
snacks of spit and spite,
dishes of delusion,
meals of "might makes right."

Let her nosh on negatives,
nurse a nagging grudge.
Hawk will soar and grow into
a fierce and ruthless judge.

Dove is love and peacefulness.
These her greatest passion.
She wants to fill the world
with loving kindness and compassion.

Let her munch on mercy,
graze on gratitude,
find flavor in forgiveness,
an accepting attitude.

She'll need a course of courage,
a piece of humble pie,
a serving of self love and care
to grow a gentle eye.

A menu made with mindfulness,
a diet of devotion,
prayer, and contemplation
will set this all in motion.

Nurture her with nature,
the sky, the sun, the earth,
drinking from the Source of life
that brought this all to birth.

Attend to her mournful cry,
heal her wounded wing,
fill her cup with gladness,
and listen to her sing!

Two birds dwelling deep within;
one coos, one squawks.
Who will have dominion—
the white dove, or the hawk?

They're settled and established.
Their nests are built to stay.
The one I feed will flourish.
Love will win the day!

Do Be Do Be Do

Do work
Be tired
Do good
Be kind
Do decide
Be wise
Do dare
Be brave
Do act
Be humble
Do speak
Be quiet
Do nothing
Be still
Do cry
Be sad
Do sing
Be happy
Do dance
Be free
Do peace
Be peace
Do love
Be love
Do Be Do Be Do

Delicate Flower

She's a delicate flower.
Life takes its toll.
A delicate flower,
body and soul.

This fast-paced world
bombarding her senses.
Each new onslaught
her whole being tenses.

Loud noises cause her
to jump with alarm.
She's ready to fight or
flee from the harm.

She needs peace and quiet,
can't take too much noise,
or she loses her center,
can't find the joys.

Her eyes appreciate
nature and art.
Keep it real, keep it simple,
or she'll fall apart.

She's freezing! She's boiling!
She feels every hurt
and can't stand a tag
anywhere on her shirt.

She gets sick from the smell
of cologne or perfume,
and she breathes in the feelings
of all in the room.

She doesn't like conflict.
Her chest squeezes tight.
Her stomach does flip-flops.
Her heart beats in fright.

The newest pandemic,
the earth's global warming,
the hatred among us,
the refugees swarming,

racial divisions,
political drama,
how does one cope in this
world full of trauma?

She carries within her
the world's heavy sorrows,
yesterday's woes,
today's, and tomorrow's.

She's a delicate flower.
Life takes its toll.
A delicate flower,
body and soul.

Fall

Safe and Sound

falling
falling
falling

we
should
have
crashed
by
now

falling
falling
falling

somehow
we're
safe
and
sound

falling
falling
falling

never
reaching
the
ground

falling
falling
falling

just
trust
the

falling
falling
falling

Fear

Fear doesn't knock,
just drops in for a visit
before I have time to ask,
"Who is it?"

She just opens the door
and moves right in
like she owns the place
taking me for a spin.

She has no boundaries.
She loves to explore
basement, hearth, attic,
every floor.

If I say, "It's time now
to pack up and go,"
she digs in her heels,
"You can't make me! No!"

The more I try to
push her out
the louder Fear
will scream and shout.

And so I'm taking
another approach
when Fear stops by
and starts to encroach.

I try not to panic.
I don't run and hide.
I open the door,
and then I confide:

"Come in! Come in!
I've missed your face.
You're welcome here,
but I'm short on space.

You see, I've welcomed in
other guests too.
So you can't just take over
when you're passing through!

Hope lives here now
with Joy and Sorrow.
It's possible Peace could
arrive here tomorrow.

Compassion and Courage
are taking up space.
And Love—Love is spreading
all over the place!

And Trust is knocking.
She'd like to live here
with her friend, Faith,
so I'll tell you what, Fear.

I'll give you a room.
Come and go as you may.
But I love my new houseguests,
and they're here to stay."

Eagle Woman

(for Laura)

My friend is gone.
Seems like yesterday.
She was an
Eagle Woman.
She was fierce,
a fighter,
brave.
She didn't let
a bald head
once covered by
braided, brown hair
deter her
or take away her
dignity.
She was beautiful,
brilliant,
articulate,
wise.
She saw things others
couldn't see.
She was
eagle-eyed.
She's soaring now.
I still miss her.

Geese

The geese passed through
on their way to somewhere new
and warm.

I watched how they flew
in their V-shaped queue,
what form!

There's wisdom in this flying crew—
lead, recede, rest, renew,
lead, recede, rest, renew,
in sun and storm.

Maybe we could take a cue,
share our journey, me and you—
lead, recede, rest, renew.
Transform.

Crow

Did you know a crow
is shiny black,
head, wings, tail,
legs, breast, and back?

Did you know a crow
is an omnivore,
eating insects, eggs, frogs,
berries, and more?

Did you know a crow
clan is called a murder,
and a birdwatching buff
is called a birder?

Did you know a crow
is oh so sociable
that congregating in a crowd
is non-negotiable?

Did you know a crow
will mate for life—
be a loyal husband
or a faithful wife?

Did you know a crow
will help dad and mother
in taking care of
younger sisters and brothers?

Did you know a crow
is super smart,
can remember a face,
tell people apart?

Did you know a crow
could be so compelling,
and all of these facts
be worthy of telling?

Well, now you know
about a crow!
Are you in awe?
Say, "Caw! Caw! "

Nuthatch Haiku

Upside down until
nuthatch gets his birdseed fill
in his pointy bill

Hollow Bone

How low must I go to be hollow?
I sigh. I cry. Hear my plea!
How low must I go to be hollow?
How high must I fly to be free?

Let go. Let go of what hinders,
trust in the Great Unknown
to make you a vessel for healing,
to make you a hollow bone.

How low must I go to be hollow?
I sigh. I cry. Hear my plea!
How low must I go to be hollow?
How high must I fly to be free?

Be open. Be spacious. Be empty.
Let fear and failure fall through.
Love will flow unencumbered.
The world needs a hollow you.

How low must I go to be hollow?
I sigh. I cry. Hear my plea!
How low must I go to be hollow?
How high must I fly to be free?

Be filled with a spirit of gladness.
Be the song only you can sing.
You are hollow, hallowed, and holy.
Look to the sky and take wing!

How low must I go to be hollow?
I sigh. I cry. Now I see!
Deeper and higher, circling wider,
Rest in the center. Just be.

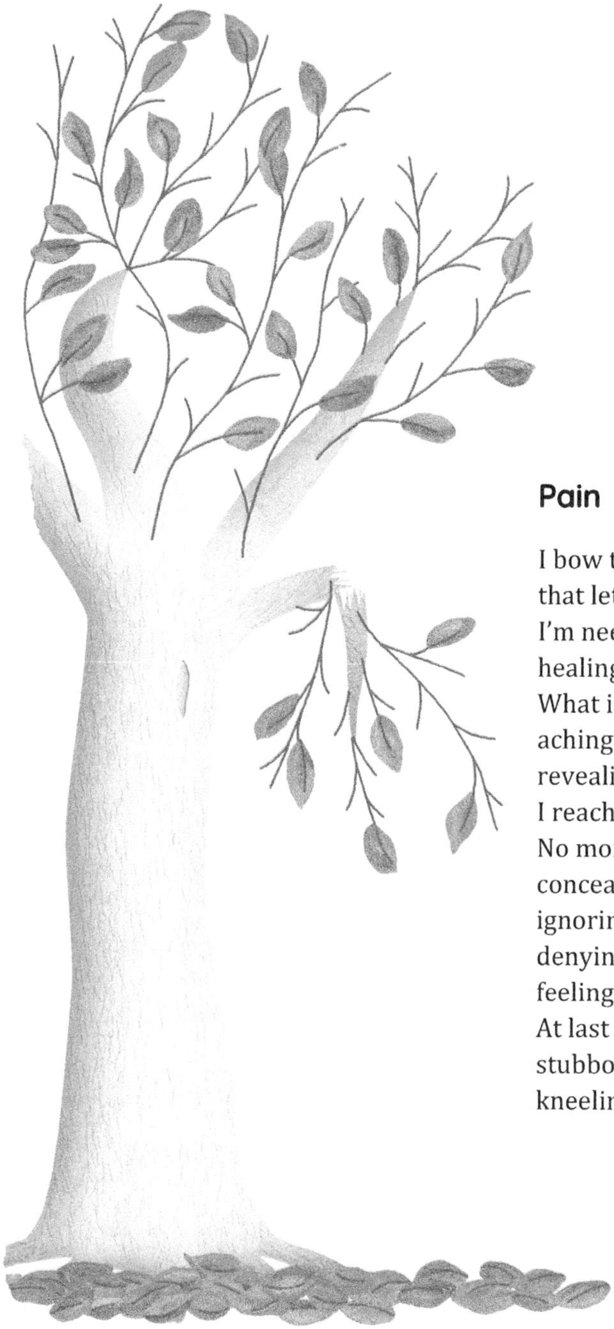

Pain

I bow to pain
that lets me know
I'm needing
healing.
What is this
aching discomfort
revealing?
I reach my limit.
No more
concealing,
ignoring,
denying the
feeling.
At last my
stubborn knees are
kneeling.

Sparrow

I'm a little brown bird,
or as birders say,
"A little brown job,"
an "LBJ."

I'm plain and humble,
browns and grays.
"Just a sparrow."
Don't get much praise.

I used to feel
that I was inferior
to other birds
with flashy exterior—

bright, blue feathers,
plump, orange breast,
wings of yellow,
deep-red crest.

I have none of their
colorful flair,
but no good comes
when I wish and compare.

I've learned over time
that I have worth
just as I am,
a gift from my birth.

My beauty's more subtle.
I may not catch your eye.
You may not take note
when I fly through the sky.

But if you come closer,
take more than a peek,
you'll see I'm amazing,
that I am unique.

Beautiful browns
in such varied hues,
chocolates, espressos,
ambers, ecrus,

color my plumage
with delicate shading,
stripes and streaks,
gradual fading.

I sing and I scratch.
I flock and I fly.
The Creator takes note
if I fall from the sky.

So don't be afraid.
Trust me, I've heard
you're loved beyond measure,
and so is this bird.

Let Go

What if
I could let go
as easily as the trees
let go in the breeze
their splendid leaves
of crimson and gold?

What if
I could let go,
just let them fall,
stand brave and tall,
naked for all
the world to behold?

What if
I could let go
the constant pursuit
to bear fruit
for the sake of repute,
let life unfold?

What if
I could let go
the fear
of losing all I hold dear,
trust spring will appear
while I wait in the cold?

What if?

What if I could?

What if I could let go?

I can.

I will.

Let go.

I will be as the trees
letting go of their leaves
of crimson and gold.

I will let them fall,
stand naked for all
the world to behold.

I'll bear fruit in due season
with love as my reason.
Let life unfold.

I'll let go the fear.
Spring will appear
with blessings untold.

Winter

Be

Be
Still
Still
Be

Be
With
Me
With
Me
Be

Be
Not
Afraid
Not
Afraid
To
Be

Wise Owl

Why's an owl called wise?
Does that come as a surprise,
or sound a bit absurd
since he's not the brightest bird?
His skill is catching prey.
He sleeps away the day.
Wise ones look for something more.
Let's go deeper. Let's explore.

Why's an owl called wise?
Maybe it's his eyes,
so human-like and forward-facing,
large and round—so all embracing,
seeing things in dark of night
that others can't in broad daylight.
Wise ones see with great precision
hearts of things with knowing vision.

Why's an owl called wise?
Could it be...did you realize
his head is capable of turning
almost fully 'round for learning
more than just one point of view:
right, left, behind, what's true?
Wise ones see with broad perspectives
unlike those a rigid neck gives.

Why's an owl called wise?
Is it his ears that maximize
his gift, exceptionally keen,
for hearing things afar, unseen?
Intently listening, quiet, mute.
When timing's right, he gives a hoot.
Wise ones listen, quiet, heedful,
only speaking when it's needful.

Why's an owl called wise?
All these reasons, I surmise.
And even though he's just a bird,
would you agree, would you concur
that people need a wise, old sage
to follow in this day and age?
Wise ones, come. Make an avowal.
Seek to learn the ways of owl.

Cheer Cheer

(for Mom and Dad)

A pair of cardinals
have made a home
in my neighborhood
and in my heart.
I've named them
Ellery and Jeanne,
these lovebirds
seldom far apart.

Mates for life
attentive to each other,
the color of love,
passion, emotion.
Together they nurture,
provide for their young—
symbol of virtue,
family devotion.

They don't fly south
for the long, harsh winter.
They weather through it
with strength, endurance—
remaining, abiding,
persevering,
ever faithful,
blessed assurance.

In joy and sorrow,
they keep on singing
their beautiful songs of
"Cheer! Cheer!"
These messengers
from beyond
bring peace and comfort,
"I'm here! I'm here!

Luggage

You left your luggage here.
What am I supposed to do with it?
Some of it is valuable.
Some of it's your shit.

It's cumbersome and heavy
and hard for me to carry.
I can't take it on my journey
even though it's necessary.

I'm already laden down
with more than I can hold;
but I love you, and I'd never
want to leave you in the cold.

So I'll leave your bags with One whose
hands can hold much more than mine,
trusting they'll be cared for
and that you, too, will be fine.

Tired

I'm so tired
of the cold.
I'm so tired
of the gray.
I'm so tired
of the blahs.
I'm so tired
of the fear.
I'm so tired
of myself.
My cold.
My gray.
My blahs.
My fear.
My uncertainty.

Junc-o

Dark-eyed Junco
Full of spunk-o
Round, gray body
Cute little chunk-o
Lifts me out of my
Winter funk-o

The Ice of March

I am walking on ice.
Would it suffice
to say I am unsteady,
unsure, unready
to live life without you?

The sky above me, clear and blue.
The mid-March sun, a golden hue.
I am oblivious, my eyes cast down
on this treacherous stretch of ground
lest I fall hard.

I don't want to be an elder yet.
I prefer being safe in the younger set.
I don't know enough. I'm so unsure.
How to live? How to endure?
I feel lost.

I want to walk a path sun-dried
with easy gait and carefree stride,
moving forward, fresh, brisk pace.
But I'm in the shadows, this icy place.
I must go slow.

Deep snow brings an end to my trail.
Do I go back? How to prevail?
I move ahead, over and through it.
A tree lends her arms of support. I knew it.
I am not alone.

The Ice of March cannot be skated
over smoothly or evaded.
The ones I loved and lost, the reason.
Spring will come in its due season.
I will wait.

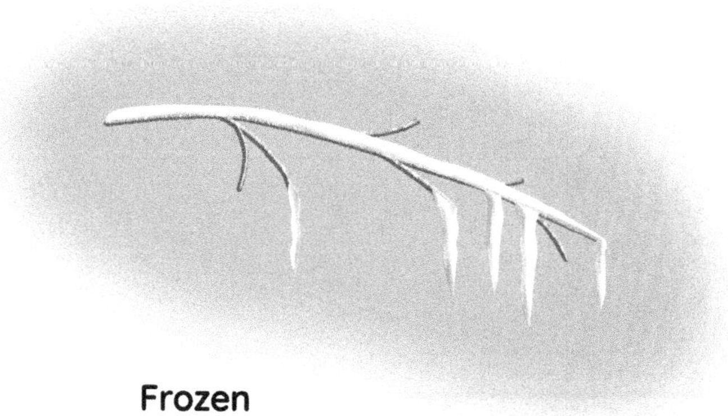

Frozen

A part of me
Is still frozen
In fear

Let it be
You are chosen
I am near

Let it go
Change is slow
You will flow

Free

Wonder

I wonder...

Can I live in wonder
without worry?

Can I allow wonder
to guide me
while I wait?

Can I withhold
from too many
whys, whens, and
what ifs?

Can I welcome
wonder
and let go of
wondering?

Can I just be
amazed at the
wonder of it all
without wallowing,
wanting,
and wishing for
what isn't?

Can I watch and
wait in wonder?

I wonder...

You Belong

He washed my feet
first one, then the other.
Poured out his love,
Jesus, my brother.

"Heed my example,
you too must do this,"
then he bent down and
tenderly gave them a kiss.

With eyes of compassion,
he looked on my face,
"You belong. Do not fear."
Then I felt his embrace.

Such kindness! Such mercy!
My sleeping heart stirred.
From within? From without?
Was that music I heard?

I wanted to dance!
Would he give it a try?
A waltz or a two-step?
I found myself shy.

We swayed for a time,
then he threw back his head
and laughed right out loud.
Then he did this instead:

His arms started flapping
as if he might fly.
Then he gestured to me
with a gleam in his eye.

"Will you partner with me?
Will you enter the dance?"
My spirit soared, and I
leapt at the chance!

We strutted, we swirled,
we stretched, and we swayed.
We pranced, and we postured.
We played as we prayed.

Our knees lifted upward.
Our heads bowed down low.
We danced with abandon,
lost in the flow.

The Word of God,
to my utter delight,
danced as a bird
with me on that night.

"Really?!" you ask.
"That just doesn't seem right!
He's far too dignified,
pious, polite!

This just can't be true.
It sounds too absurd!
The Holy One never
would dance like a bird!"

I know it seems strange
that Jesus and I
were busting out moves
ere he went forth to die.

But this was his farewell
message for me:
"Don't take life
quite so seriously!

Yes, life is hard, but
keep singing this song.
Do not fear. I am with you.
My love, you belong.

Keep loving, keep serving
with heart open wide.
Keep dancing! And don't lose
your fun, playful side!"

New Spring

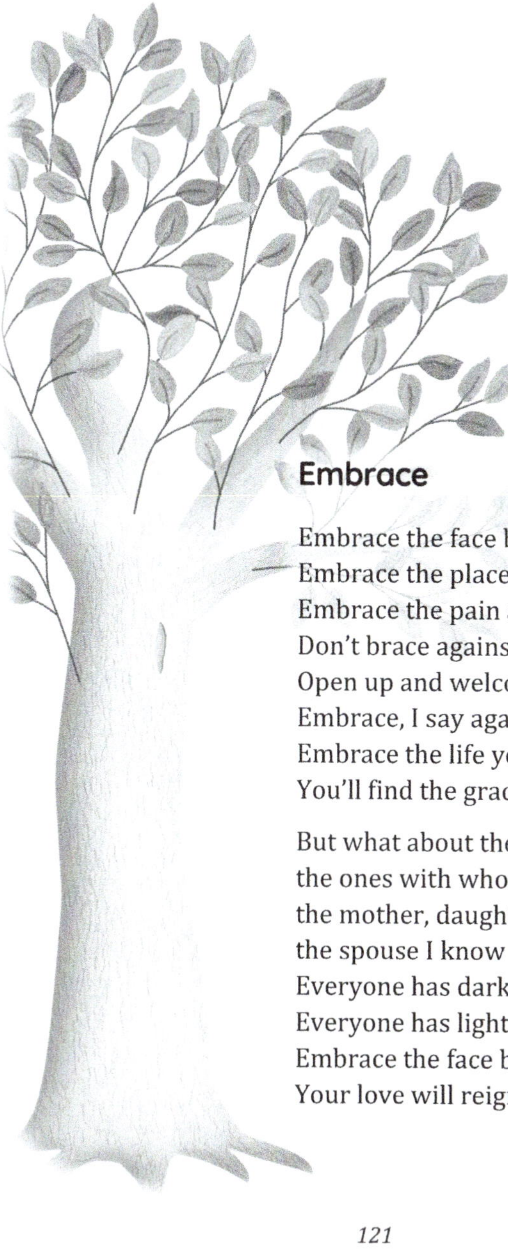

Embrace

Embrace the face before you.
Embrace the place you're in.
Embrace the pain and sorrow.
Don't brace against today, tomorrow.
Open up and welcome in.
Embrace, I say again.
Embrace the life you're living.
You'll find the grace therein.

But what about the people,
the ones with whom I dwell,
the mother, daughter, brother,
the spouse I know so well?
Everyone has darkness.
Everyone has light.
Embrace the face before you.
Your love will reignite.

And what about my fears,
the ones that keep me wide awake,
the fear of faults and failures,
rejection and heartache?
Embrace your imperfections.
Embrace the you you are.
Dare to live and dare to love.
You're worthy of the scar.

And what about the questions
that keep circling undefined?
I'd like to know the answers.
I'd like some peace of mind.
Birth, death, heaven, hell,
beauty, evil, strife?
Embrace the deep unknowing
of this mystery we call life.

And what about the here and now,
the place I'm in today?
Can I accept this moment
and not try to run away
from tragedy or triumph,
the inspiring or mundane?
Embrace it all, embrace it *all*,
the sunshine and the rain.

Embrace the face before you.
Embrace the place you're in.
Embrace the pain and sorrow.
Don't brace against today, tomorrow.
Open up and welcome in.
Embrace, I say again.
Embrace the life you're living.
You'll find the grace therein.

I Am

I am
tired of
pretending
I am
more than
I am.

I am
tired of
pretending
I am
less than
I am.

I am
(more or less)
who
I am.

Receive

What is it you want?
Ask. Believe.
In gratitude open
your heart. Receive.

Asking takes courage.
Admitting your needs
and hurts is humbling,
but everyone bleeds.

There's joy for the asking,
love freely given
within you, around you.
Time to start livin'.

Rise from your sleep.
Awaken. Perceive.
Be vulnerable. Open
your heart. Receive.

Am I There Yet?

I'd like to say
I've arrived.
For so long
I've strived
to know,
to be sure,
to be right,
to quell the fright
of being wrong,
imperfect,
in darkness,
not light.
I'd like to have it
all figured out,
the Mystery solved.

But what would be the point?
To know it all?
No one likes a know-it-all
who thinks she's better than,
above it all!
Is the knowing
really the call?
No! Not at all!
No one knows it all.
Only the All in All knows all.
So trust the here, the now,
not there, not how.
The point isn't
the knowing.
It's the growing
in Love.

Love is the journey,
the goal, the prize.
But please know
you'll never realize
it all.
So stop this striving
and thoughts of arriving.
Do not fear.
It's clear we're here
to grow in love
year after year after
year after year.
And the All in All
who is Love is near
as we flourish,
as we fall.

Spring Mantra

Inhale: love is in the air
Exhale: don't despair
Inhale: it's here, there
Exhale: everywhere
Inhale: breathe in a prayer
Exhale: breathe out and share
Inhale: love is in the air

Chickadee

Chicka-dee-dee-dee
Chicka-dah-dah-dah
Chicka-dee Chicka-dah
Chicka-tra-la-la

Little round body
Little white tum
Little black cap
Chicka-rum-pum-pum

Chicka-dee-dee-dee
Chicka-doo-doo-doo
Chicka-dee Chicka-doo
Chicka-I-Love-You

Meadowlark's Message

Standing alone on precarious perch
overlooking the native prairie,
I lift my head to the open skies,
I open my throat and ferry
a golden song o'er waves of grain
and grasses straight to thee,
struggling to keep your head afloat,
awash in your stormy sea
of doubt, overwhelm, indecision,
on precarious perch of your own.
Will you heed and take hold of this lifeline,
which I so sweetly intone?

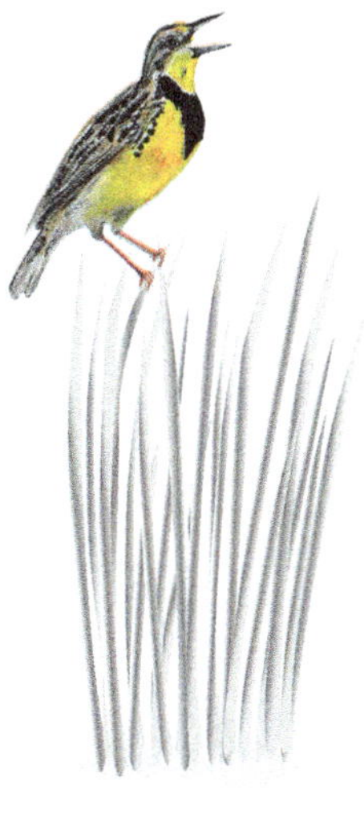

"Joy, joy, joy," I sing!
Faith! Have faith, my dear.
"Abundance, abundance, abundance," I bring!
The time for rejoicing is near!
The seeds have been sown in the depths of your heart.
You weeded and watered. They grew.
The harvest is ready and meant to be shared.
This bounty is not just for you.
I know you would rather stay hidden.
You're afraid if you really succeed,
judgment will come, unbidden.
Will you be enough? Will you have what you need?

"Trust, trust, trust," I trill!
Trust this song compelling
you to leave your ego in the nest
and trust Divine Indwelling.
You trusted, just trusted the falling.
But now I'm here advising,
release what's keeping you buried in fear;
you must trust, just trust the rising.
There was safety in the shadows,
but I need you here in the light.
I was with you in the falling;
I'll be with you in the flight.

"Soar, soar, soar," I flute!
Soar to the ends of the earth!
Spread this message as old as time,
this message of death and rebirth.
Join me in scattering hope and joy,
warmth to a weary world.
The time is nigh to take the leap
and spread your wings unfurled!
Love will surely lift you.
Love is in the air.
Assent to the ascent.
I am here. I am there.

Epilogue

Birds of a Feather

Birds of a feather
flocking together,
a beautiful sight to see.
Sharing, surviving,
everyone thriving,
how lovely when all agree.

But there's flack in the flock,
and a duck on the dock,
who's odd as odd can be,
and a peacock who's proud,
and a crow who's too loud,
and an eagle looks down from his tree.

Is there room in the nest
for those not like the rest?
Can I love those who think unlike me?
In this world that's gone wrong,
may all beings belong
and stretch out their wings to fly free.

Acknowledgments

I love the quiet, contemplative and introspective process of writing poetry. But the challenge of publishing a book of poetry was quite an overwhelming endeavor for me, requiring a completely different set of skills and mindset than my usual way of being and operating in the world. Upon staring out my window one day, I found myself watching the squirrels and rabbits at my bird feeder. I was struck by the thought that even though I was more like the timid bunny, sneaking out to nibble at the crumbs on the ground, this publishing business was going to require me to become more like the tenacious and daring squirrel. I later wrote that I would need to:

> Take a lesson from the squirrel who feeds
> at your delicatessen of suet and seeds,
> relentlessly
>
> Obstacles arise but he is nonplussed,
> his eye on the prize, and full of trust
> in his ability.
>
> He lets his ego take a rest.
> With a leap says, "Here we go!" to reach his quest.
> Invariably,
>
> he'll succeed. After many, many tries
> he'll feast on seeds and actualize
> abundance and prosperity!

I did take a lesson from that squirrel, but unlike he in his solo attempts, I could not have done it alone. *Time to Soar* would never have come to fruition without the love, support and help from these very special people in my life:

First and foremost, I want to thank Mary Jo Savageau, my cousin and illustrator, for collaborating with me on this book. I remember sitting with her at my table, at what seems like an eternity ago, telling her about my book idea and asking for technical help. While Mary Jo drew the perfect little sketch, we were both struck by the feeling that a collaboration between us was meant to be. We learned through some difficult trials that we had to be vulnerable, trust one another, and speak our own truth with honesty and love. We promised and stood by our resolve to never let a disagreement threaten our relationship. This book would never have been published without Mary Jo's vast expertise in all things computer. Her artwork is brilliant and brings an added depth and cohesiveness to the whole book. I am beyond grateful. What a gift to be reunited with her, to join our talents and souls together to create something so beautiful!

Another integral person who I owe a deep amount of gratitude to is Trish Tallakson. I do believe God brought us together. How else could I have gotten a counselor, spiritual director, art and dance lover, life coach, cheerleader, and book editor all wrapped up in the same person? Her interest in and response to my poetry inspired me to keep writing. She was the one who first suggested I choreograph and dance my poems. I would never have had the courage or confidence to pursue this journey without her guidance, encouragement, wisdom, and insight. She believed in me when I didn't believe in myself.

Last, but not least, I am so grateful for my loving and supportive circle of family and friends. My husband, Mike, is the most loyal person I know. He is also the most patient person I know—which is especially good for me when I'm in the middle of a creative project and forget about practical things like buying groceries and paying bills. I am ever grateful for his acceptance, support, and abiding love. My daughter, Kellie Knodel, is the squirrel of the family. I am inspired by her courage, confidence, and passion. She has nurtured my heart and helped me to soar. My sons, Philip and Danny, are engaged in their own creative pursuits. Their commitment to their passions and dreams inspire me to keep developing and sharing my own gifts. My sisters Joan, Mary, Susan, Teresa, and all those sisters from other mothers, too numerous to mention, are who I rely on for prayer, friendship and support. Their love lifts me.

I am also grateful to my brothers, Mike, Tom, and Pat, and the rest of my extended family who have been the first fans of my many poems, skits and performances over the years. I love a receptive audience who appreciates my gifts! And my parents, Ellery and Jeanne, who gave me my roots and taught me what was important in life. Their love is ever with me.

In addition to this book of poetry, many of my poems have been put into dance and are available to view either in a performance setting or on my website: www.worddances.com

I would like to thank Barb Wieland, my cousin and fellow dancer/choreographer for joining me in this endeavor. We have danced together since childhood, so partnering again at this stage in our lives to choreograph and perform these word dances has been a joy and godsend! Her dancing is still as exquisite and graceful as ever and a beautiful addition to my poetry.

And finally, I would like to thank God and these beautiful birds for building their nest within me and singing the songs I needed to hear.

About the Author and Illustrator

Photo by Noah Kupcho

Katie Bruckbauer

Katie was raised on a farm outside of Casselton, ND. She grew up in a large, faith-filled family full of kindness and compassion, safety and security, pride and perfection. Katie considers herself a recovering perfectionist, and is awakening to the idea that life is really most beautiful in its imperfections. She is practicing patience as this slow process to freedom unfolds.

Katie finds poetry to be a healing avenue for exploring the complexities, questions, hardships, joys, and beauty of life. Her poetry is influenced by her extensive background in modern dance and creative movement. Katie loves to play with the symbols and sounds, rhythm and rhyme, subtleties and surprises of word in verse form. Wisdom, whimsy, and wonder flow through her, dancing on the page, joining her heart with fellow travelers on the human journey.

Katie lives in Fargo with her husband, Mike. They have 3 adult children and live next door to their 3 grandchildren.

For further inspiration, visit worddances.com to view performance videos of her poetry in motion or to purchase artwork.

Mary Jo Savageau

Mary Jo grew up not far from her cousin Katie. She loved art from an early age and has always been fascinated by what can emerge from lines and color on a blank piece of paper. She studied both art and English in college, and, after many years working in communications fields, she started Wide Open Skies Creative Services doing web design and consulting. She illustrated *Time to Soar* with a combination of watercolor paintings and digital art.

Mary Jo and her husband, John, live in Bismarck, ND, and have two daughters. Visit her site at wideopenskies.com.

Made in the USA
Monee, IL
18 March 2024

54692860R00089